Englisch-Stars

4

Für Profis

Erarbeitet von

Jasmin Brune
Daniela Elsner
Stefanie Gleixner-Weyrauch
Marion Lugauer
Sabine Schwarz

Illustriert von
Barbara Jung
Thilo Pustlauk
Wilfried Poll

Cornelsen

Inhalt

 Comic

The class picture

Class 4a, please come to the blackboard. Mr. Smile wants to take a picture of our class.

Psst! Take a pencil! When the photographer says „Cheese!", put the pencil under your nose!

Say „Cheese!"

Ha, ha, great picture!

Ha, ha!

Three days later, the class gets their class picture. Everyone likes it...

... except Mary.

Oh no!

Don't be sad. I've got a pen to make you happy again,...

... but next time, just smile!

1. True or false? Tick ✓.

	true	false
Mary is in class 4a.	◯	◯
The photographer wants to take a class picture.	◯	◯
The photographer's name is Mr. Cheese.	◯	◯
Mary wants the other pupils to put a rubber under their nose.	◯	◯
All the pupils put pencils under their noses.	◯	◯
Mary isn't very happy when she sees the picture.	◯	◯
Mary's teacher says "Next time, just sleep."	◯	◯

Richtig oder falsch? Mache einen Haken.

one   two   three   four   five   six   seven   eight   nine   ten
eleven   twelve   thirteen   fourteen   fifteen   sixteen   seventeen
eighteen   nineteen   twenty   thirty   forty   fifty   sixty   seventy
eighty   ninety   one hundred

What time is it? It's … o'clock. It's … 15/30/45. It's quarter past/half past/quarter to …

2. Read and draw lines.

Let's take a picture.

It's three thirty.

Ten, twenty, thirty, forty, fifty, sixty, seventy.

Welcome back to school!

What time is it, please?

Ordne die Sprech-blasen dem richti-gen Bild zu.

3. What time is it? Colour.

3.30 / half past three

1.00 / one o'clock

8.15 / quarter past eight

2.45 / quarter to three

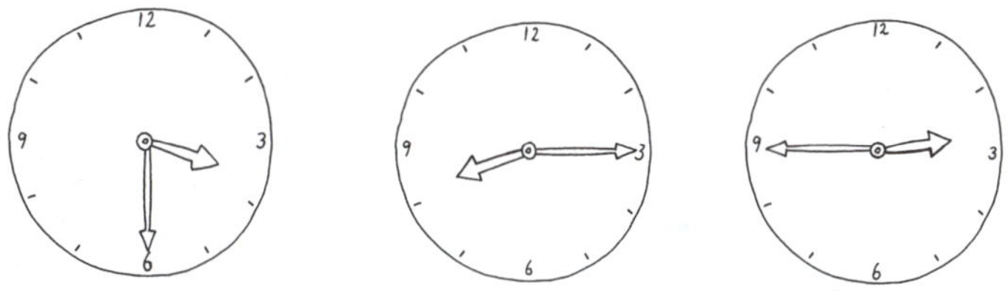

Male jeweils die Uhr und die passende Uhrzeit in der gleichen Farbe an.

4. Read and write.

One, three, five, _____, _____

Ten, twenty, forty, _____, _____

Two, twenty, three, thirty, four, _____, _____,

_____, _____, _____,

_____, _____, _____, _____

One hundred, ninety, eighty, _____, _____, _____

Five, ten, fifteen, twenty, _____, _____, _____

Führe die Zahlen-reihen weiter.

5

🔊 Comic

A very special home

Schau dir den Comic nochmal an und vervollständige die Sätze.

 1. Read and fill in the missing words.

There is a cheap _____ in the newspaper. It's _____

per month. The living room looks like a _____. The bathroom

looks like a _____. The kitchen looks like a _____.

The bedroom is in the _____.

They all think the house is too _____ for them.

2. Find the words. Write.

Welche Möbelstücke haben sich hinter dieser Geheimschrift versteckt? Falls du Hilfe brauchst schaue im Wörterkasten nach.

attic   bathroom   bedroom
car   cellar   furniture
garage   garden   kitchen
living room   toilet   bed
chair   lamp   shelves
sofa   stairs   table
wardrobe   too big
too small   just right

to belong in – hineingehören

to call – anrufen

cheap – billig

to look like – aussehen wie

lovely – schön

newspaper – Zeitung

per month – pro Monat

special – besonders

to stay – bleiben

3. Draw lines. Write the words in alphabetical order.

Ordne die Bilder den Wörtern zu und schreibe sie dann in alphabetischer Reihenfolge auf.

stairs

attic

cellar

bedroom

kitchen

living room

toilet

bathroom

attic, _____

_____

4. Too big, too small or just right? Tick ✓.

Schaue dir die Bilder an und entscheide ob die Möbelstücke zu groß, zu klein oder genau richtig sind.

The chair is
○ too small
○ too big
○ just right.

The shelves are
○ too small
○ too big
○ just right.

The wardrobe is
○ too small
○ too big
○ just right.

5. Look at the pictures. What's wrong? Circle what does not belong in the room. Fill in the missing words.

The <u>sofa</u> doesn't belong in the

<u>bathroom</u>.

It belongs in the _____.

The _____ doesn't belong in the

_____. It belongs in the

_____.

The _____ doesn't belong in the

_____. It belongs in the

_____.

The _____ doesn't belong in the

_____. It belongs in the

_____.

The _____ doesn't belong in the

_____. It belongs in the

_____.

Irgendwas stimmt hier nicht. Wie gehört es richtig? Kreise ein, was falsch ist und vervollständige die Sätze

9

 Comic

Sam's job

Delivering newspapers is so boring!

This is the perfect job for me.

BOB'S DINER

BOB'S DINER
Help wanted!

Can I help you?

Yes, I'd like chicken and chips and a glass of lemonade, please.

Here's your fish and chips and your glass of coke.

Sorry, but that's wrong! I ordered chicken and chips and a glass of lemonade.

Here's your tomato soup, your carrot salad and your orange juice.

Sorry, but that's wrong! We ordered carrot soup, a tomato salad and two glasses of apple juice!

Okay Sam, you better clear the tables!

Oh no, the plates and glasses!

YOU'RE FIRED!

Delivering newspapers is the best job for me!

10

1. True or false? Tick ✓.

	true	false
Sam is a girl.	◯	◯
He has got a green bike.	◯	◯
He gets a new job at a diner.	◯	◯
The boy in the diner orders chicken and chips.	◯	◯
The girls in the diner order carrot soup, a tomato salad and orange juice.	◯	◯
The forks and knives fall down.	◯	◯
Sam isn't good at his job at the diner.	◯	◯

lunch   chicken
chips   fish   ham
hamburger   hot dog
mashed potatoes
pizza   salad
sandwich   sausage
soup   spaghetti
coke   orange juice
water   cup   fork
glass   knife – knives
plate   spoon   diner
restaurant

boring –
  langweilig
to clear the table –
  den Tisch ab-
  räumen
to deliver news-
  papers – Zeitun-
  gen austragen
to order – bestellen

Help wanted! –
  Aushilfe gesucht!
You're fired! –
  Du bist gefeuert!

2. What do they want to order? Look and write.

Wenn man etwas bestellen möchte, sagt man höflich: *I'd like … (a hamburger), please. I'd* ist die Abkürzung für *I would.*

I'd like sausages with mashed potatoes and a glass of coke, please.

I'd like _____

_____

_____

_____

_____

_____

_____

_____

_____

_____

_____

_____

✏ 3. What do they say? Write the dialogue.

 Frage, ob du helfen kannst.

_____

 Bejahe und bestelle eine Pizza und ein Glas Cola.

_____

 Gib das Essen und sage wieviel es kostet.

_____

 Gib das Geld und verabschiede dich.

_____

 Bedanke dich und verabschiede dich.

_____

Can I help you?

Yes, I'd like a pizza and a glass of coke, please.

Thank you. Bye.

Here your are. Goodbye.

Here you are. That's £4.50.

Die Sprechblasen helfen dir!

13

 Comic

Let's get fit

1. Find the adjectives.

For Sally...

snowboarding is too _____.

playing hockey is too _____.

doing yoga is _____.

swimming is too _____.

riding is too _____.

to play the recorder / piano / guitar / saxophone

to play tennis / football / hockey / handball / basketball

to dance   to do judo / gymnastics / yoga   to ice skate

to inline skate   to read books   to run   to swim   to skateboard

to sing   to ride a bike / a horse

I can / I can't...

I like / I don't like...

too cold – zu kalt

too dangerous – zu gefährlich

too difficult – zu schwierig

to feel good – sich wohlfühlen

relaxing – entspannend

too wet – zu nass

That's what I want! – Das möchte ich!

2. What are their hobbies? What do they like?

Emily likes playing the recorder and _____

_____.

Sam likes _____ and

_____.

Jane _____ _____

and _____.

Jack _____ _____

and _____.

Schau dir die Bilder an und schreibe auf, welche Hobbies die Kinder ausüben.

Joe _____ _____,

_____ and

_____.

3. Answer the questions. Write.

Wenn du sagst, dass du eine Sportart ausüben kannst, sagst du: I can …, z.B.: I can swim. Das Verb bleibt hier unverändert.

 Yes, I can.

 No, I can't.

Can you play the guitar? _____

Can you snowboard? _____

Can you play football? _____

Can you play the piano? _____

Can you swim? _____

Can you play tennis? _____

Can you dance? _____

4. What are your hobbies? Write.

Wenn vor dem -y ein Konsonant steht wird daraus im Plural ein –ie, z.B. hobby – hobbies

_____

_____

_____

_____

My hobbies are yoga and skipping rope.

 Comic

A day in the life of Sally and Max

Good morning!

Sally gets up at 7 o'clock in the morning.

It's time to get up.

Max gets up at 7 o'clock in the evening.

Let's jump up high.

For Sally school starts at 8 o'clock in the morning.

Look. You have special hands. You can fly with them.

For Max school starts at 8 o'clock in the evening.

Yippee!!! No home-work today.

For Sally school ends at 3 o'clock in the afternoon.

Hurray, school is over!!!

For Max school ends at 3 o'clock in the morning.

Let's play pouchball.

Sally plays with her friends at 5 o'clock in the afternoon.

Catch me if you can.

Max plays with his friends at 5 o'clock in the morning.

I like lollipops.

Sally has dinner at 6.15 in the evening.

I like insects.

Max has dinner at 6.15 in the morning.

Good night!

Sally goes to bed at 8 o'clock in the evening.

I'm so tired.

Max goes to bed at 8 o'clock in the morning.

1. Tick ✓ the correct sentence and find the missing word.

Max gets up at 7 o'clock in the morning. ☐ h
Max gets up at 7 o'clock in the afternoon. ☐ a
Max gets up at 7 o'clock in the evening. ☐ t

For Sally school ends at 3 o'clock in the afternoon. ☐ i
For Sally school starts at 3 o'clock in the afternoon. ☐ a
For Sally school ends at 3 o'clock in the morning. ☐ n

Sally plays basketball with her friends. ☐ g
Sally plays pouchball with her friends. ☐ r
Sally plays baseball with her friends. ☐ p

Max has dinner at 6.15 in the morning. ☐ e
Max has dinner at 6.30 in the morning. ☐ p
Max has dinner at 6.15 in the evening. ☐ r

Sally goes to football training at 8 o'clock in the evening. ☐ y
Sally goes to school at 8 o'clock in the evening. ☐ y
Sally goes to bed at 8 o'clock in the evening. ☐ d

Sally is _____ in the morning.

morning   afternoon   evening
night   weekend
to do homework   to get up
to go to bed   to go to school
to have breakfast / lunch / dinner
to play   to read a book
to sleep   to watch TV

insects –
   Insekten
pouch – Beutel
to catch – fangen

 2. Read and fill in.

Normally, animals go to sleep in the _____. But some animals

_____ in the evening and go to sleep in the _____.

Bats are active _____. When you _____ at 8 o'clock,

these animals are already asleep. And when you _____ with your

friends at 4 o'clock the bats still sleep. But when you _____ in

the evening, then all these animals get up and look for _____.

go to bed morning get up go to school	
at night food play evening	

3. Read the questions and answer.

When do you get up on a
school day?
On a school day I get up at

_____.

When do you get up on the
weekends?
On the weekends I get up at

_____.

When do you come home from
school?
I come home from school at

_____.

When do you have lunch?
I have lunch at

_____.

When do you do your homework?
I do my homework at

_____.

When do you play with your friends?
I play with my friends at

_____.

When do you go to bed on the
weekends?
On the weekends I go to bed at

_____.

4. Make sentences. Write them in the order of your daily routine.

Bilde Sätze und ordne sie nach deinem Tagesablauf.

In the morning	I go to bed.
At lunchtime	I get up.
In the afternoon	I go to school.
In the evening	I play with my friends.
At night	I do my homework.
	I have dinner.
	I play the piano/guitar/…
	I read a book.
	I watch TV.
	I have lunch.

_____

_____

_____

_____

_____

_____

📖 👂 Comic

The shopping list

It's Saturday morning.

We need cheese, bananas and butter.

cheese bananas butter

Sally, can you go to the shopping centre, please? The shopping list is in the basket.

No problem.

cheese bananas butter

Sally is going shopping.

Bye! And don't forget anything.

Goodbye!

Suddenly it's starting to rain.

Oh, no!

Shopping centre

At the shopping centre.

Supermarket Shoes Sport

I can't read what's on the list.

Look, Mum! I've got chocolate, a basketball and a pullover.

Oh Sally!

1. Read the comic again. Write the shopping lists.

Mum's shopping list:

Was steht auf der Einkaufsliste? Und was hat Sally stattdessen gekauft?

ch _ _ _ _

ba _ _ _ _ _

_ _ _ _ er

But this is what Sally brings home: _____,

a _____ and a _____.

2. Odd one out. Cross out the word that doesn't match.

apple	chocolate	lemonade	shoes
cherry	cheese	doll	trousers
strawberry	biscuits	ball	book
spinach	ice cream	teddy bear	pullover

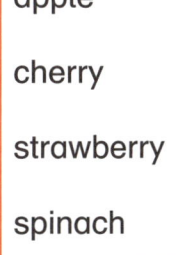

apple   basket   biscuit   to buy   cheese   cherry   chocolate
egg   fruit   ham   honey   ice cream   lemonade   milk   new
orange juice   pear   plum   shopping list   spinach   strawberry
sweets   vegetables   book shop   clothes shop   pharmacy
restaurant   shoe shop   shopping centre   sports shop
supermarket   sweets shop   too small   too big   just right   perfect
I like it.   How much is it?

3. Read the shopping lists. Draw lines.

biscuits	spinach	strawberries	pineapple
cheese	honey	cherries	lemons
eggs	apples	eggs	apple juice
ice cream	ham	spinach	jam
	lemonade		

4. Correct the sentences. Cross out and write.

I can buy inline skates in the ~~book shop~~ sports shop .

I can buy apples in the pharmacy _____.

I can buy books in the shoe shop _____.

I can buy pizza in the clothes shop

_____.

I can buy boots in the supermarket

_____.

Wo kann man die Dinge kaufen? Streiche das falsche Geschäft durch und schreibe das richtige auf.

Liebe Kinder,

herzlichen Glückwunsch! Ihr habt nun schon so viel Englisch gelernt, dass Ihr ganz alleine mit den Englisch-Stars für Profis arbeiten könnt.

In diesem Heft findet Ihr 12 lustige, spannende und interessante Geschichten im Comicformat und zahlreiche Übungen und Rätsel rund um das Thema der Geschichten.

Was kannst du mit diesem Heft machen?

– Nimm dir dieses Heft im Unterricht immer dann, wenn du mit deinen Aufgaben schon fertig bist, oder zu Hause, wenn du noch mehr üben willst. Denn du weiß ja: Übung macht den Meister.

– Suche dir zunächst den Comic heraus, der am besten zu dem Thema passt, das Ihr gerade im Unterricht behandelt. Also z. B. „Shopping" oder „Transport". Ein kleines Zeichen (Icon) am oberen Ende der Seite zeigt dir das Thema an.

– Lies den Comic entweder zunächst alleine durch oder gemeinsam mit einem Partner. Die meisten Wörter in den Comics dürftest du kennen. Solltest

du ein Wort mal nicht verstehen, dann versuche es dir über die Bilder oder den Kontext zu erschließen. Wenn das nicht klappt, dann kannst du im „Wörterbuch" auf der nächsten Seite nachsehen. Dort findest du die Übersetzungen für unbekannte Wörter.

Du kannst dir die Comics auch anhören. Bitte deine Eltern dafür die Audio-Dateien aus dem Internet herunterzuladen.

– Anschließend bearbeitest du die nachfolgenden Seiten mit den Übungen. Fange hier am besten immer mit der ersten Übung an, denn in dieser kannst du feststellen, ob du den Comic richtig verstanden hast, oder ob du ihn besser nochmal liest.

– Mit dem Lösungsheft kannst du nachsehen, ob du alle Aufgaben richtig gelöst hast.

Und zum Schluss möchte sich noch Willi, der schlaue Wurm bei dir vorstellen. Er begleitet dich, neben Sally dem Känguru, in diesem Heft und erinnert dich an wichtige Regeln im Englischen oder gibt dir Tipps.

Informationen für Eltern und Lehrkräfte:

Liebe Eltern, liebe Lehrkräfte,

die Englisch Stars für Profis sind als differenzierendes Material für Schülerinnen und Schüler gedacht, die schon gut mit der englischen Sprache zurechtkommen, und etwas mehr üben möchten. Da im Unterricht oft wenig Zeit zum selbstständigen Lesen bleibt, das Lesen aber ein wichtiger Bestandteil des Fremdsprachenlernens ist, sollen die Englisch Stars für Profis diese Lücke schließen. Jedes Kapitel beginnt deshalb mit einem thematisch zum Unterricht passenden Comic. Diese sollen von den Kindern alleine oder gemeinsam mit einem Partner gelesen werden. Die meisten Wörter in den Comics sind bekannt. Unbekannte Wörter erschließen sich die Kinder aus dem Kontext. Ebenfalls wird eine Übersetzung neuer Wörter angeboten. Die Comics finden Sie auch als Audio-Dateien zum herunterladen unter **www.oldenbourg.de/englisch-stars-profis-audio-4**.

Weitere Aussprachehilfen bieten die gängigen digitalen Vokabeltrainer und Wörterbücher.

Fragen zum Text und weitere Übungen, zur Festigung von Vokabeln, zum Leseverstehen, Schreiben und zum Sprechen folgen den Geschichten.

Nach dem Lesen und der Bearbeitung der Aufgaben können sich die Kinder Belohnungssterne ins Heft kleben.

Das integrierte Lösungsheft ermöglicht die Selbstkontrolle.

Willi der Wurm begleitet die Kinder und gibt wichtige Tipps und Hinweise.

Die Englisch Stars für Profis sind die optimale Vorbereitung für die weiterführende Schule.

Lösungen

1. True or false? Tick ✓.

	true	false
Mary is in class 4a.	✓	
The photographer wants to take a class picture.	✓	
The photographer's name is Mr. Cheese.		✓
Mary wants the other pupils to put a rubber under their nose.		✓
All the pupils put pencils under their noses.		✓
Mary isn't very happy when she sees the picture.	✓	
Mary's teacher says "Next time, just sleep."		✓

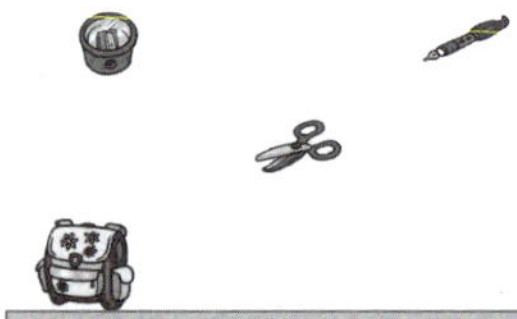

Richtig oder falsch? Mache einen Haken.

one two three four five six seven eight nine ten
eleven twelve thirteen fourteen fifteen sixteen seventeen
eighteen nineteen twenty thirty forty fifty sixty seventy
eighty ninety one hundred
What time is it? It's ... o'clock. It's ... 15/30/45. It's quarter past/
half past/quarter to ...

2. Read and draw lines.

Ordne die Sprechblasen dem richtigen Bild zu.

Let's take a picture.

It's three thirty.

Ten, twenty, thirty, forty, fifty, sixty, seventy.

Welcome back to school!

What time is it, please?

3. What time is it? Colour.

(rot) 3.30 / half past three
(blau) 1.00 / one o'clock
(gelb) 8.15 / quarter past eight
(grün) 2.45 / quarter to three

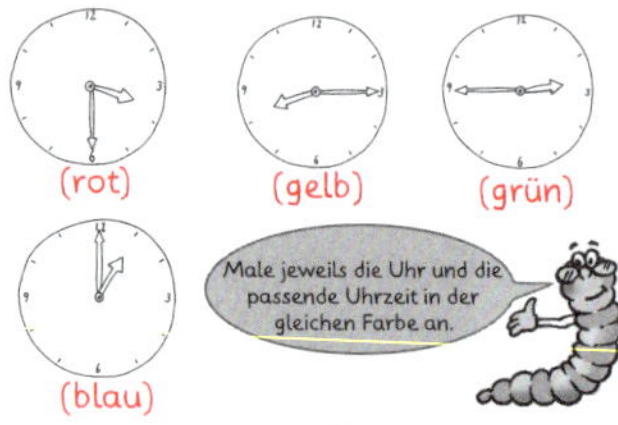

(rot)   (gelb)   (grün)

(blau)

Male jeweils die Uhr und die passende Uhrzeit in der gleichen Farbe an.

4. Read and write.

Führe die Zahlenreihen weiter.

One, three, five, seven, nine

Ten, twenty, forty, sixty, eighty

Two, twenty, three, thirty, four, forty, five,
fifty, six, sixty,
seven, seventy, eight, eighty

One hundred, ninety, eighty, seventy, sixty, fifty

Five, ten, fifteen, twenty, twenty-five, thirty, thirty-five

Comic

A very special home

Wow, this is a very cheap house! Maybe this will be our new home! Let's look at it.

DAILY NEWS
Looking for a new home? We have the perfect house for you.
It's only £ 333 per month.
Call: 444 444
A-2 REAL ESTATE

Let's go in!

This is the lovely living room.

Living room? But this looks like a bathroom.

This is the lovely bathroom.

Bathroom? But this looks like a kitchen.

This is the lovely kitchen.

Kitchen? But this looks like a bedroom.

This is the lovely bedroom.

Bedroom? But this is the garden.

It's a lovely house. Do you like it?

Well, we think it's too special for us. We want to stay in our lovely house.

Schau dir den Comic nochmal an und vervollständige die Sätze.

1. Read and fill in the missing words.

There is a cheap house in the newspaper. It's £ 333 per month. The living room looks like a bathroom. The bathroom looks like a kitchen. The kitchen looks like a bedroom. The bedroom is in the garden. They all think the house is too special for them.

2. Find the words. Write.

Welche Möbelstücke haben sich hinter dieser Geheimschrift versteckt? Falls du Hilfe brauchst schaue im Wörterkasten nach.

t a b l e   s h e l v e s   l a m p   c h a i r

attic bathroom bedroom
car cellar furniture
garage garden kitchen
living room toilet bed
chair lamp shelves
sofa stairs table
wardrobe too big
too small just right

to belong in – hineingehören
to call – anrufen
cheap – billig
to look like – aussehen wie
lovely – schön
newspaper – Zeitung

per month – pro Monat
special – besonders
to stay – bleiben

🖊 3. Draw lines. Write the words in alphabetical order.

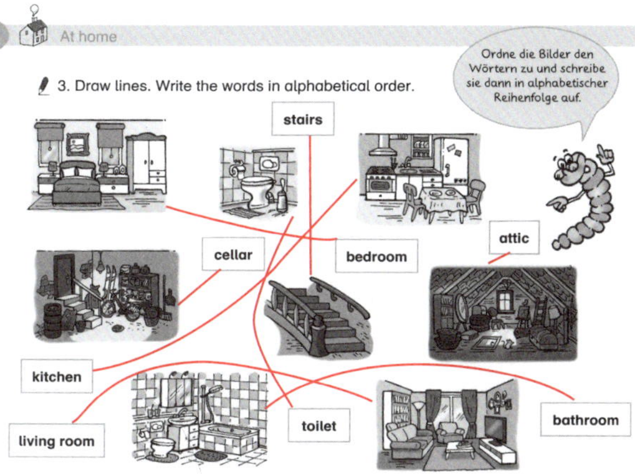

Ordne die Bilder den Wörtern zu und schreibe sie dann in alphabetischer Reihenfolge auf.

stairs

cellar

bedroom

attic

kitchen

living room

toilet

bathroom

attic, bathroom, bedroom, cellar, kitchen, living room, stairs, toilet

🖊 4. Too big, too small or just right? Tick ✓.

Schaue dir die Bilder an und entscheide ob die Möbelstücke zu groß, zu klein oder genau richtig sind.

The chair is
○ too small
✓ too big
○ just right.

The shelves are
○ too small
○ too big
✓ just right.

The wardrobe is
✓ too small
○ too big
○ just right.

8

🔍🖊 5. Look at the pictures. What's wrong? Circle what does not belong in the room. Fill in the missing words.

The sofa doesn't belong in the bathroom.
It belongs in the living room.

The table doesn't belong in the bedroom. It belongs in the kitchen / living room.

The bed doesn't belong in the cellar. It belongs in the bedroom.

The toilet doesn't belong in the garden. It belongs in the bathroom.

The car doesn't belong in the living room. It belongs in the garage.

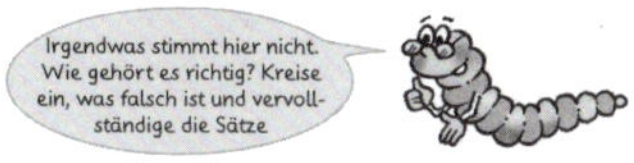

Irgendwas stimmt hier nicht. Wie gehört es richtig? Kreise ein, was falsch ist und vervollständige die Sätze.

9

📖🔊 Comic

Sam's job

Delivering newspapers is so boring!

This is the perfect job for me.

BOB'S DINER

BOB'S DINER Help wanted!

Can I help you?

Yes, I'd like chicken and chips and a glass of lemonade, please.

Here's your fish and chips and your glass of coke.

Sorry, but that's wrong! I ordered chicken and chips and a glass of lemonade.

Here's your tomato soup, your carrot salad and your orange juice.

Sorry, but that's wrong! We ordered carrot soup, a tomato salad and two glasses of apple juice!

Okay Sam, you better clear the tables!

Oh no, the plates and glasses!

YOU'RE FIRED!

Delivering newspapers is the best job for me!

10

🖊 1. True or false? Tick ✓.

	true	false
Sam is a girl.	○	✓
He has got a green bike.	✓	○
He gets a new job at a diner.	✓	○
The boy in the diner orders chicken and chips.	✓	○
The girls in the diner order carrot soup, a tomato salad and orange juice.	○	✓
The forks and knives fall down.	○	✓
Sam isn't good at his job at the diner.	✓	○

lunch   chicken
chips   fish   ham
hamburger   hot dog
mashed potatoes
pizza   salad
sandwich   sausage
soup   spaghetti
coke   orange juice
water   cup   fork
glass   knife – knives
plate   spoon   diner
restaurant

boring – langweilig

to clear the table – den Tisch abräumen

to deliver newspapers – Zeitungen austragen

to order – bestellen

Help wanted! – Aushilfe gesucht!

You're fired! – Du bist gefeuert!

11

Lösungen

Wenn man etwas bestellen möchte, sagt man höflich: I'd like ... (a hamburger), please. I'd ist die Abkürzung für I would.

🔍✏️ 2. What do they want to order? Look and write.

I'd like sausages with mashed potatoes and a glass of coke, please.

I'd like a sandwich with chips and a glass of water, please.

I'd like a pizza, a salad and a glass of coke, please.

I'd like a tomato soup, chicken with chips and a glass of orange juice, please.

✏️ 3. What do they say? Write the dialogue.

BOB'S DINER - MENU
pizza · salad · cola
fish & chips · sandwich · orange juice
· · water

Frage, ob du helfen kannst.
Can I help you?

Bejahe und bestelle eine Pizza und ein Glas Cola.
Yes, I'd like a pizza and a glass of coke, please.

Gib das Essen und sage wieviel es kostet.
Here you are. That's £ 4,50.

Gib das Geld und verabschiede dich.
Here you are. Goodbye.

Bedanke dich und verabschiede dich.
Thank you. Bye.

Can I help you?
Here your are. Goodbye.
Die Sprechblasen helfen dir!
Yes, I'd like a pizza and a glass of coke, please.
Thank you. Bye.
Here you are. That's £4.50.

📖🎵 Comic

Let's get fit

Feel good! Do sports!

That's what I want!

I don't like playing hockey. It's too difficult for me.

I don't like swimming. It's too wet for me.

I don't like riding. It's too dangerous for me.

I don't like snowboarding. It's too cold for me.

I love doing yoga! It's very relaxing. It's not too difficult, not too wet, not too dangerous, not too cold. It's just right for me!

✏️ 1. Find the adjectives.

For Sally...

snowboarding is too **cold**

playing hockey is too **difficult**

doing yoga is **just right**

swimming is too **wet**

riding is too **dangerous**

to play the recorder / piano / guitar / saxophone
to play tennis / football / hockey / handball / basketball
to dance   to do judo / gymnastics / yoga   to ice skate
to inline skate   to read books   to run   to swim   to skateboard
to sing   to ride a bike / a horse
I can / I can't...
I like / I don't like...

too cold – zu kalt
too dangerous – zu gefährlich
too difficult – zu schwierig
to feel good – sich wohlfühlen

relaxing – entspannend
too wet – zu nass
That's what I want! – Das möchte ich!

✏️ 2. What are their hobbies? What do they like?

Emily likes playing the recorder and **hockey**

Sam likes **reading books** and **riding a horse**.

Jane **likes singing** and **ice skating**.

Jack **likes swimming** and **riding a bike**.

Joe **likes playing tennis**, **playing football** and **playing the guitar.**

Schau dir die Bilder an und schreibe auf, welche Hobbies die Kinder ausüben.

16

✏️ 3. Answer the questions. Write.

Wenn du sagst, dass du eine Sportart ausüben kannst, sagst du: I can ..., z.B.: I can swim. Das Verb bleibt hier unverändert.

Yes, I can.   No, I can't.

Can you play the guitar? _____

Can you snowboard? _____

Can you play football? _____

Can you play the piano? _____ **(individuelle Lösung)**

Can you swim? _____

Can you play tennis? _____

Can you dance? _____

✏️ 4. What are your hobbies? Write.

Wenn vor dem -y ein Konsonant steht wird daraus im Plural ein -ie, z.B. hobby – hobbies

_____
(individuelle Lösung)
_____

My hobbies are yoga and skipping rope.

17

📖 🎵 Comic

A day in the life of Sally and Max

Good morning!

It's time to get up.

Sally gets up at 7 o'clock in the morning.

Max gets up at 7 o'clock in the evening.

Let's jump up high.

Look. You have special hands. You can fly with them.

For Sally school starts at 8 o'clock in the morning.

For Max school starts at 8 o'clock in the evening.

Yippee!!! No homework today.

Hurray, school is over!!!

For Sally school ends at 3 o'clock in the afternoon.

For Max school ends at 3 o'clock in the morning.

Let's play pouchball.

Catch me if you can.

Sally plays with her friends at 5 o'clock in the afternoon.

Max plays with his friends at 5 o'clock in the morning.

I like lollipops.

I like insects.

Sally has dinner at 6.15 in the evening.

Max has dinner at 6.15 in the morning.

Good night!

I'm so tired.

Sally goes to bed at 8 o'clock in the evening.

Max goes to bed at 8 o'clock in the morning.

18

✏️ 1. Tick ✓ the correct sentence and find the missing word.

Max gets up at 7o'clock in the morning. [h]
Max gets up at 7o'clock in the afternoon. [a]
Max gets up at 7o'clock in the evening. [✓]

For Sally school ends at 3 o'clock in the afternoon. [✓]
For Sally school starts at 3 o'clock in the afternoon. [a]
For Sally school ends at 3 o'clock in the morning. [n]

Sally plays basketball with her friends. [g]
Sally plays pouchball with her friends. [✓]
Sally plays baseball with her friends. [p]

Max has dinner at 6.15 in the morning. [✓]
Max has dinner at 6.30 in the morning. [p]
Max has dinner at 6.15 in the evening. [r]

Sally goes to football training at 8 o'clock in the evening. [y]
Sally goes to school at 8 o'clock in the evening. [y]
Sally goes to bed at 8 o'clock in the evening. [✓]

Sally is **tired** in the morning.

morning   afternoon   evening
night   weekend
to do homework   to get up
to go to bed   to go to school
to have breakfast / lunch / dinner
to play   to read a book
to sleep   to watch TV

insects – Insekten
pouch – Beutel
to catch – fangen

19

2. Read and fill in.

Lies den Text und setze die Wörter ein.

Normally, animals go to sleep in the **evening**. But some animals **get up** in the evening and go to sleep in the **morning**. Bats are active **at night**. When you **go to school** at 8 o'clock, these animals are already asleep. And when you **play** with your friends at 4 o'clock the bats still sleep. But when you **go to bed** in the evening, then all these animals get up and look for **food**.

| go to bed | morning | get up | go to school |
| at night | food | play | evening |

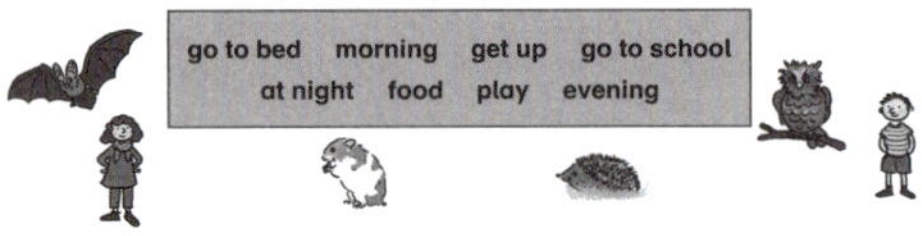

3. Read the questions and answer.

When do you get up on a school day?
On a school day I get up at
_____

When do you get up on the weekends?
On the weekends I get up at

When do you come home from school?
I come home from school at

When do you have lunch?
I have lunch at
_____.

When do you do your homework?
I do my homework at
_____

When do you play with your friends?
I play with my friends at
_____

When do you go to bed on the weekends?
On the weekends I go to bed at

Wie sehen deine Tage so aus? Beantworte die Fragen.

(individuelle Lösung)

20

4. Make sentences. Write them in the order of your daily routine.

Bilde Sätze und ordne sie nach deinem Tagesablauf.

In the morning
At lunchtime
In the afternoon
In the evening
At night

I go to bed.
I get up.
I go to school.
I play with my friends.
I do my homework.
I have dinner.
I play the piano/guitar/…
I read a book.
I watch TV.
I have lunch.

In the morning I get up / go to school.
At lunchtime I have lunch.
In the afternoon I do my homework / play with my friends / play the piano … / read a book / watch TV. In the evening I have dinner / watch TV / read a book. At night I go to bed.

21

Comic

The shopping list

It's Saturday morning.

We need cheese, bananas and butter.

Sally, can you go to the shopping centre, please? The shopping list is in the basket.

No problem.

Sally is going shopping.

Bye! And don't forget anything.

Goodbye!

Suddenly it's starting to rain.

Oh, no!

Shopping centre

At the shopping centre.

I can't read what's on the list.

Look, Mum! I've got chocolate, a basketball and a pullover.

Oh Sally!

22

1. Read the comic again. Write the shopping lists.

Was steht auf der Einkaufsliste? Und was hat Sally stattdessen gekauft?

Mum's shopping list:

ch **e e s e**
ba **n a n a s**
butt er

But this is what Sally brings home: **chocolate**, a **basketball** and a **pullover**.

2. Odd one out. Cross out the word that doesn't match.

apple	chocolate	lemonade	shoes
cherry	cheese	doll	trousers
strawberry	biscuits	ball	book
spinach	ice cream	teddy bear	pullover

apple   basket   biscuit   to buy   cheese   cherry   chocolate
egg   fruit   ham   honey   ice cream   lemonade   milk   new
orange juice   pear   plum   shopping list   spinach   strawberry
sweets   vegetables   book shop   clothes shop   pharmacy
restaurant   shoe shop   shopping centre   sports shop
supermarket   sweets shop   too small   too big   just right   perfect
I like it.   How much is it?

23

Shopping

3. Read the shopping lists. Draw lines.

| biscuits cheese eggs ice cream | spinach honey apples ham lemonade | strawberries cherries eggs spinach | pineapple lemons apple juice jam |

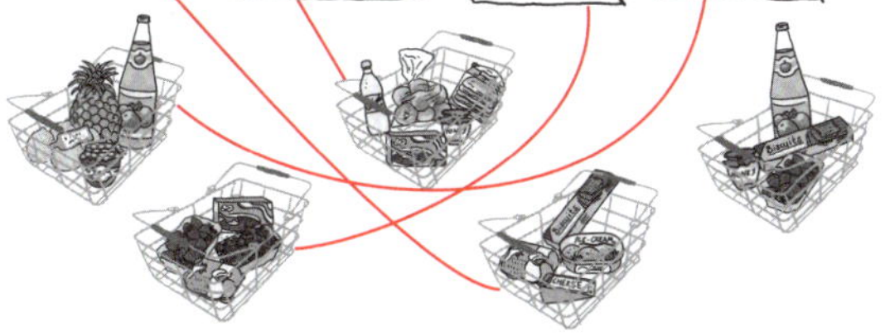

4. Correct the sentences. Cross out and write.

I can buy inline skates in the ~~book shop~~ sports shop.

I can buy apples in the ~~pharmacy~~ supermarket.

I can buy books in the ~~shoe shop~~ book shop.

I can buy pizza in the ~~clothes shop~~ supermarket/restaurant.

I can buy boots in the ~~supermarket~~ shoe shop.

Wo kann man die Dinge kaufen? Streiche das falsche Geschäft durch und schreibe das richtige auf.

Shopping

5. Fill in the speech bubbles.

It's too big. | I like it. | It's too small.

I don't like it. | I like it. | It's too big. | It's too small. | I don't like it.

Welche Aussage passt zu welchem Bild? Trage in die Sprechblasen ein.

6. Read the dialogue. Find the correct order and number.

5 Try this one.
6 It's perfect. I like it. How much is it?
2 Hi. I'd like a new pullover.
4 I like it. But it's too small.
1 Hello. Can I help you?
9 Thank you. Bye.
7 It's 12 pounds.
8 Here you are.
10 Bye.
3 Here are the pullovers. Try them on.

Bringe den Dialog in die richtige Reihenfolge und nummeriere.

Transport

Comic

How do I get to school?

Stop! Wait for me! | Oh no! How do I get to school now?
I can't take the plane to school. | I can't take the train to school.
I can't take the ferry to school. | I've got an idea!
Koala, stop! Wait for me! Can you take me to school on your bike, please? | A bike is perfect to get to school!

Transport

1. Read the sentences. Fill in the gaps.

Sally is late. She misses the (school) bus.

She can't get to school by plane, by train or by ferry.

Sally's friend Koala gets to school by bike.

For Sally and Koala a bike is perfect to get to school.

2. Look at the picture. What different vehicles can you see? Count and write.

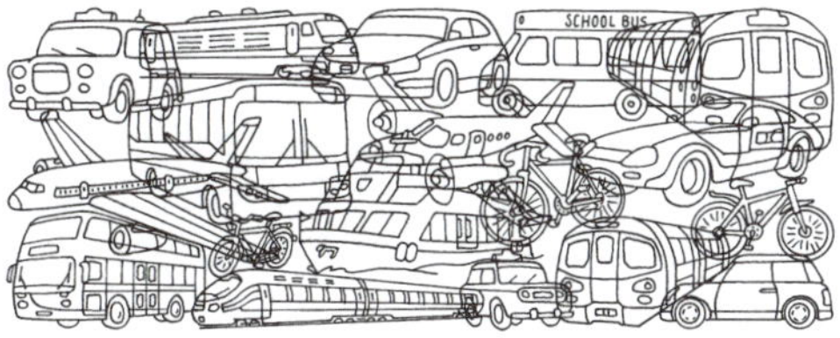

I can see 3 cars, 2 taxis, 2 trains, 2 undergrounds, 3 bikes, 1 school bus, 2 planes, 1 ferry.

Zähle die verschiedenen Fahrzeuge und schreibe auf.

bike boat bus – buses car ferry – ferries plane taxi train underground

to get to – hinkommen
to miss – verpassen
to take – nehmen
vehicle – Fahrzeug
to wait – warten

Lösungen

3. Look at the pictures. Write the sentences.

The fish gets to school by **ferry**
The dog gets **to school by car**.
The frog **gets to school by plane**.
The hamster **gets to school by train**.
The cat **gets to school by underground**.
The guinea pig **gets to school by taxi**.
Sally **gets to school by bike**.

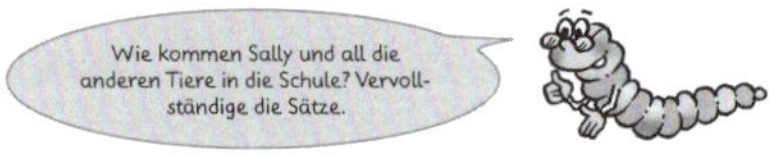

Wie kommen Sally und all die anderen Tiere in die Schule? Vervollständige die Sätze.

---

4. Make dialogues. Write.

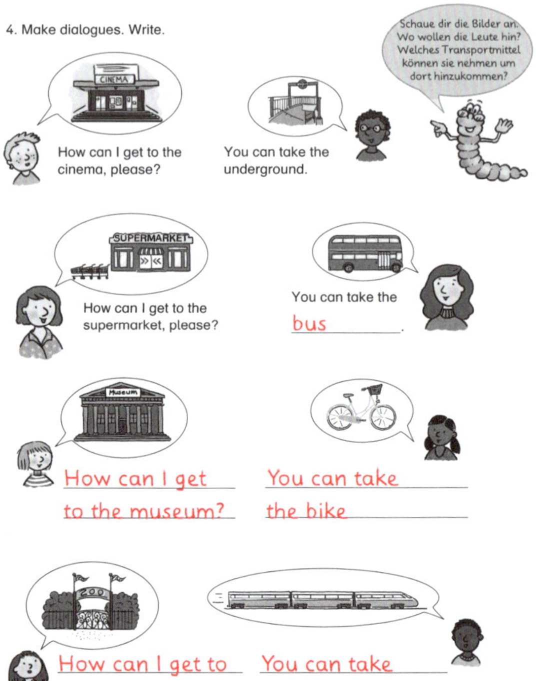

Schaue dir die Bilder an. Wo wollen die Leute hin? Welches Transportmittel können sie nehmen um dort hinzukommen?

How can I get to the cinema, please? — You can take the underground.

How can I get to the supermarket, please? — You can take the **bus**.

How can I get to the museum? — **You can take the bike**

How can I get to the zoo? — **You can take the train.**

Comic

Good friends

A DAY IN THE JUNGLE

The tortoise is reading a book.

The fat hippo is swimming in the river.

The strong elephant is lifting heavy weights.

It's so boring here. Every day is the same.

The tall giraffe is eating leaves off the tree.

The dangerous lion is frightening the zebra. The fast zebra is running away.

The monkey is right. Every day is the same.

But what can we do?

I've got an idea.

THE NEXT DAY

The clever tortoise is eating leaves off the tree.

The hippo is reading a book and the giraffe is swimming in the river.

The long snake is lifting heavy weights.

Hey friends, what are you doing?

The fast zebra is frightening the dangerous lion. The dangerous lion is running away.

We want to make you laugh.

You are so crazy! You are my best friends!

---

1. Look at the end of the comic. What are the animals doing? Read and draw lines.

The snake — is swimming in the river.
The giraffe — is eating leaves off the tree.
The lion — is reading a book.
The zebra — is running away.
The tortoise — is frightening the lion.
The hippo — is lifting heavy weights.

Two animals are missing. Write.

elephant, monkey

animal elephant	behind – hinter	to lift – heben
giraffe hippo jungle	boring – langweilig	to run away – wegrennen
lion monkey parrot	to frighten – erschrecken	sharp – scharf
river snake tortoise	heavy – schwer	to weigh – wiegen
tree zebra clever	high – hoch	weights – Gewichte
dangerous fast fat	in front of – vor	
funny long old	leaves – Blätter	
strong tall		
in on under		

Wild animals (page 32)

2. Read and find the adjective.

The elephant can lift about 300 kilogrammes.
The elephant is __strong__.

The hippo weighs about 1500 kilogrammes.
The hippo is __fat__.

The zebra can run about 75 kilometres per hour. The zebra is __fast__.

The tortoise lives about 150 years.
The tortoise is __old__.

The lion has got sharp teeth.
The lion is __dangerous__.

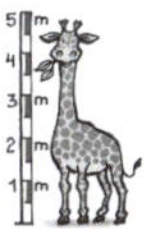

The giraffe is about 5 metres high. The giraffe is __tall__.

| dangerous |
| old   tall |
| strong |
| fast   fat |

3. Which word is wrong? Cross it out.

The lion is the ~~banana~~ king of the jungle.
The elephant is ~~in~~ big and strong.
The crocodile is very ~~hot~~ dangerous.
The snake is very long ~~hair~~.

The monkey likes to swing ~~songs~~ in the trees.
The tortoise ~~drinks~~ eats grass.
The hippo swims in the river ~~salt~~.
The ~~dog~~ parrot flies from tree to tree.

32

Wild animals (page 33)

4. Where are the animals? Write.

rock

bush

| in   on   under   behind   next to   in front of |

The monkey is in the tree.
The hippo is __in the river.__
The giraffe is in front of the tree.
The zebra is behind the tree.
The tortoise is next to the bush.
The lion is on the rock.
The snake is under the rock.
The parrot is on the hippo.

33

At the doctor's (page 34)

Comic

Sally at the dentist

What's the matter Sally?

I've got a toothache.

Open your mouth.

You've got a hole in your tooth.

bzzzz

Finished!

Sally, brush your teeth at least in the morning and in the evening.

Don't eat too many sweets. Bacteria like the sugar on your teeth. They attack your teeth.

But I don't eat sweets. I only eat lollipops.

Oh Sally! No more lollipops for you. Here is a toothbrush and toothpaste for you.

34

At the doctor's (page 35)

1. Read and circle the wrong word. Write the correct word.

I've got a ~~headache~~. __toothache__

You have got a hole in your ~~foot~~. __tooth__

Open your ~~nose~~. __mouth__

Bacteria like the sugar on your ~~mouth~~. __teeth__

Brush your ~~hair~~ at least in the morning and in the evening. __teeth__

Here is a ~~shoe brush~~ and toothpaste for you. __toothbrush__

| arm   broken   ear – earache   eye   finger   foot – feet |
| head – headache   to hurt   knee   leg   mouth   nose |
| to open   stomach – stomachache   throat – sore throat |
| tooth – teeth   toothache   What's the matter? |

bacteria – Bakterien	toothbrush – Zahnbürste
to brush – bürsten	toothpaste – Zahnpasta
hole – Loch	

Achte auf den unregelmäßigen Plural:
one tooth – two teeth
one foot – two feet

35

Lösungen

2. Find the 6 differences. Circle and write.

In picture 1 the zebra has got a headache. In picture 2 the zebra has got a stomachache.

In picture 1 the hippo has got a toothache. In picture 2 *the hippo has got a toothache.*

In picture 1 the lion has got a headache.
In picture 2 the lion has got a toothache.
In picture 1 the elephant has got a broken arm.
In picture 2 the elephant has got an earache.
In picture 1 the giraffe has got a stomachache.
In picture 2 the giraffe has got a sore throat.
In picture 1 the tortoise has got a sore throat.
In picture 2 the tortoise has got a broken arm.

36

3. What's the matter? Look and write.

 I've got a *sore throat* .

 My *finger* hurts.

 I've got a *headache* .

 My *knee* hurts.

4. Read and number in the correct order.

4	Is my leg broken?
2	My leg hurts.
6	Thank you Doctor Miller.
3	Okay, let's see.
5	No, your leg isn't broken. Let's put some ice on it.
7	See you again next week.
1	What's the matter with you?

37

Comic

A long day

38

1. True or false? Tick ✓.

	true	false
Oscar has to do his homework.	✓	
Oscar has to make his bed.		✓
Oscar has to help in the garden.		✓
Oscar has to take the cat for a walk.		✓
Oscar has to clean the kitchen.	✓	
Oscar has to feed the cat.	✓	
Oscar plays football in the afternoon.		✓

doctor   gardener   hairdresser   pilot
policeman / policewoman   shop assistant
teacher   to babysit   to do homework
to feed the cat   to help in the garden
to make breakfast
to make my bed   to tidy my room
to walk the dog   to work

to have to – müssen

late – spät

mess – Durcheinander

You have no idea! – Du hast keine Ahnung!

39

Jobs

2. What do these children have to do in the house? Look and write.

I have to __make my bed__

I have to __help in the garden__

I have to __babysit__

I have to __make breakfast__

I have to __tidy my room__

3. What are their jobs? Find the words.

I'm a __hairdresser__ — radesrehsri

I'm a __policeman__ — lmcipnoea

I'm a __teacher__ — acereht

I'm a __pilot__ — otipl

Jobs

4. Where do they work? Draw lines and write.

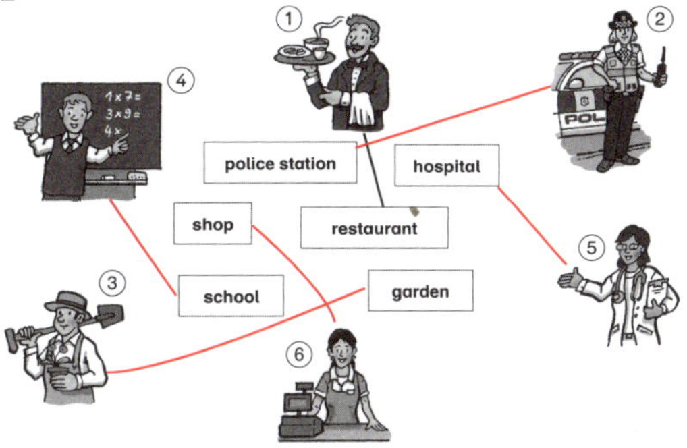

police station · hospital · shop · restaurant · school · garden

① __The waiter works at the restaurant.__
② __The policewoman works at the police station.__
③ __The gardener works in the garden.__
④ __The teacher works at the school.__
⑤ __The doctor works in the hospital.__
⑥ __The shop assistant works at the shop.__

5. What do you want to be? Draw and write.

(individuelle Lösung)   I want to be a

40   41

Meeting people

Comic

The new pupil

Good morning everybody. This is Dimitri, our new pupil. He is from Greece. He has lived in many countries.

Group Work! 1) List 5 countries in Europe. Name the capital cities, too.

I know France and Spain. But what are the capital cities? Any idea? ????

Can we google them?

Stop. I know it. Paris is the capital city of France and Madrid is the capital city of Spain.

I know Denmark and Italy. But what are the capital cities? Any idea? ???

Can we google them?

Stop! I know it. The capital city of Denmark is Copenhagen and the capital city of Italy is Rome.

We know Croatia and Poland. But we don't know the capital cities. Can we google them?

You don't have to google them. Just ask Dimitri!

Meeting people

1. Look at the comic. Write the countries.

Finde die Länder zu diesen Hauptstädten.

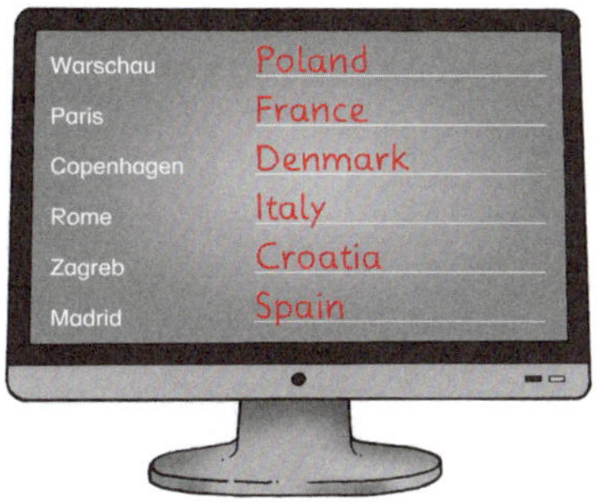

Warschau	__Poland__
Paris	__France__
Copenhagen	__Denmark__
Rome	__Italy__
Zagreb	__Croatia__
Madrid	__Spain__

Dimitri is from __Greece__. The capital city is __Athens__.

capital city city – cities country – countries Croatia Denmark
England France Germany Great Britain Greece Italy
Poland Spain Sweden Turkey English French German
Greek Spanish Turkish Ankara Athens Berlin Copenhagen
London Madrid Paris Rome Stockholm Warschau Zagreb
Where are you from? – I'm from ...
Which languages can you speak? – I (can) speak ...

42   43

Lösungen

Kennst du die Länder und ihre Hauptstädte? Die Abbildungen, die typisch für die entsprechenden Länder sind helfen dir dabei.

✏ 2. Do you know these countries? Write.

Map with: Sweden, Great Britain, Germany, France, Spain, Italy, Turkey

What are their capital cities?

🦌 Stockholm   🏛 London

🐄 Berlin   💃 Madrid

🍝 Rome   ☪ Ankara

🗼 Paris

44

✏ 4. Which languages do the children speak? Write.

Hi. I'm Susana. I'm from Sp**ain**. I speak **Spanish**.

Hi. I'm Tom. I'm from **England**. I speak **English**.

My name is Burak. I'm from **Turkey**. I speak **Turkish**.

Bonjour! My name is Celine. I'm from **France**. I speak **French**.

Now it's your turn.

(individuelle Lösung)

My name is _____. I'm from _____. I speak
_____. I can also speak _____.

📖✏ 5. Read. Colour the question and the correct answer in the same colour.

Hi! What's your name? (blau)

I'm from Greece. (gelb)

I speak Greek. (grün)

Can you speak any other languages? (rot)

Where are you from? (gelb)

My name is Dimitri. (blau)

Male die Frage und die passende Antwort in derselben Farbe an.

Yes, I can speak English, too. (rot)

Which language do you speak? (grün)

45

📖🎧 Comic

The Little Indian Boy

Once upon a time there lived an Indian family in a tepee, an Indian tent.

They all had Indian names. My name is Singing Bird. I love to sing.

And my name is Fast Horse. I can run very fast.

My name is Little Rainbow because I love colours.

I'm strong like a bear. That's why my name is Strong Bear.

Our baby is born! Come here everybody. Our little boy needs a name.

Was it a dark night when he was born? No!

Was it snowy and cold when he was born? No!

Was it rainy or cloudy when he was born? No!

Little Rainbow and Strong Bear had a little baby boy.

But the sun was shining when he was born. That's a perfect name for our little boy: Shining Sun!

Welcome to our family, Shining Sun!

46

📖✏ 1. Read and tick ✓ the correct answer.

What is a tepee?
☑ It's an Indian tent. ☐ It's an Indian horse.

Whose name is Fast Horse?
☐ It's Grandma's name. ☑ It's Grandpa's name.

Why is Dads's name Strong Bear?
☑ Because he is strong like a bear. ☐ Because he is brown like a bear.

What was the weather like when the little boy was born?
☐ It was a cold and dark night. ☑ It was a warm and sunny day.

Ein indianischer Name hatte immer eine besondere Bedeutung. Er richtete sich z.B. nach einer körperlichen Eigenschaft, einer Ähnlichkeit mit einer Pflanze oder einem Tier oder aber nach einem Wetterereignis am Tag der Geburt.

American football
California   cowboy   Florida
Hollywood   Indian
New York
president   ranch
Statue of Liberty
White House

background – Hintergrund
to be born – geboren werden
famous – berühmt
popular – beliebt

president – Präsident
stripes – Streifen
tent – Zelt
tepee – Indianerzelt

47

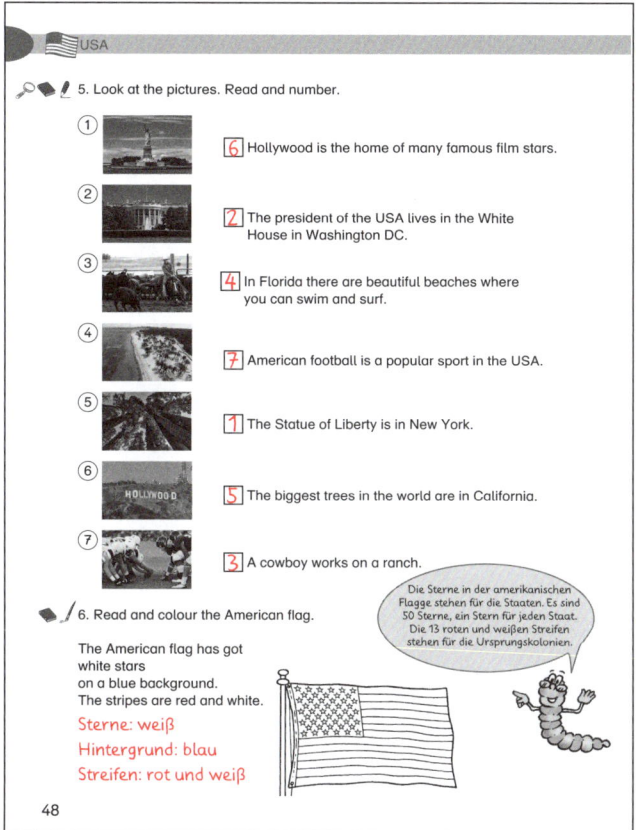

Hast du Sally gefunden? Sie hat sich auf Seite 11, 19, 33 und auf Seite 47 versteckt.

Illustrationen:

Barbara Jung: S. 7, S. 11, S. 14, S. 16, S. 17, S. 18, S. 20, S. 21, S. 22, S. 23, S. 24, S. 25, S. 26, S. 28, S. 29, S. 34, S. 36, S. 37, S. 40 (Aufgabe 3), S. 41, S. 43 (Flaggen), S. 46, S. 47

Thilo Pustlauk: S. 3, S. 4, S. 5 (Aufgabe 2), S. 6, S. 8, S. 9, S. 10, S. 12, S. 13, S. 27, S. 30, S. 31, S. 32, S. 33, S. 38, S. 40 (Aufgabe 2), S. 41, S. 42, S. 43, S. 44, S. 45, S. 46, S. 48

Wilfried Poll: S. 5 (Aufgabe 3), S. 11 (Sally), S. 19 (Sally), S. 33 (Sally), S. 39, S. 47 (Sally)

Wurm: Thilo Pustlauk

Kapitelvignetten: Wilfried Poll

Icons Wörterkästen: Thilo Pustlauk

Icons Aufgabenanweisungen: Wilfried Poll, Barbara Jung (Buch, Lupe)

Welche Aussage passt zu welchem Bild? Trage in die Sprechblasen ein.

_____

ber.

u. Bye.

ounds.

Hi. I'd like a new pullover.

I like it. But it's too small.

Hello. Can I help you?

Here you are.

Bye.

Here are the pullovers. Try them on.

Bringe den Dialog in die richtige Reihenfolge und nummeriere.

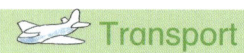

Comic

How do I get to school?

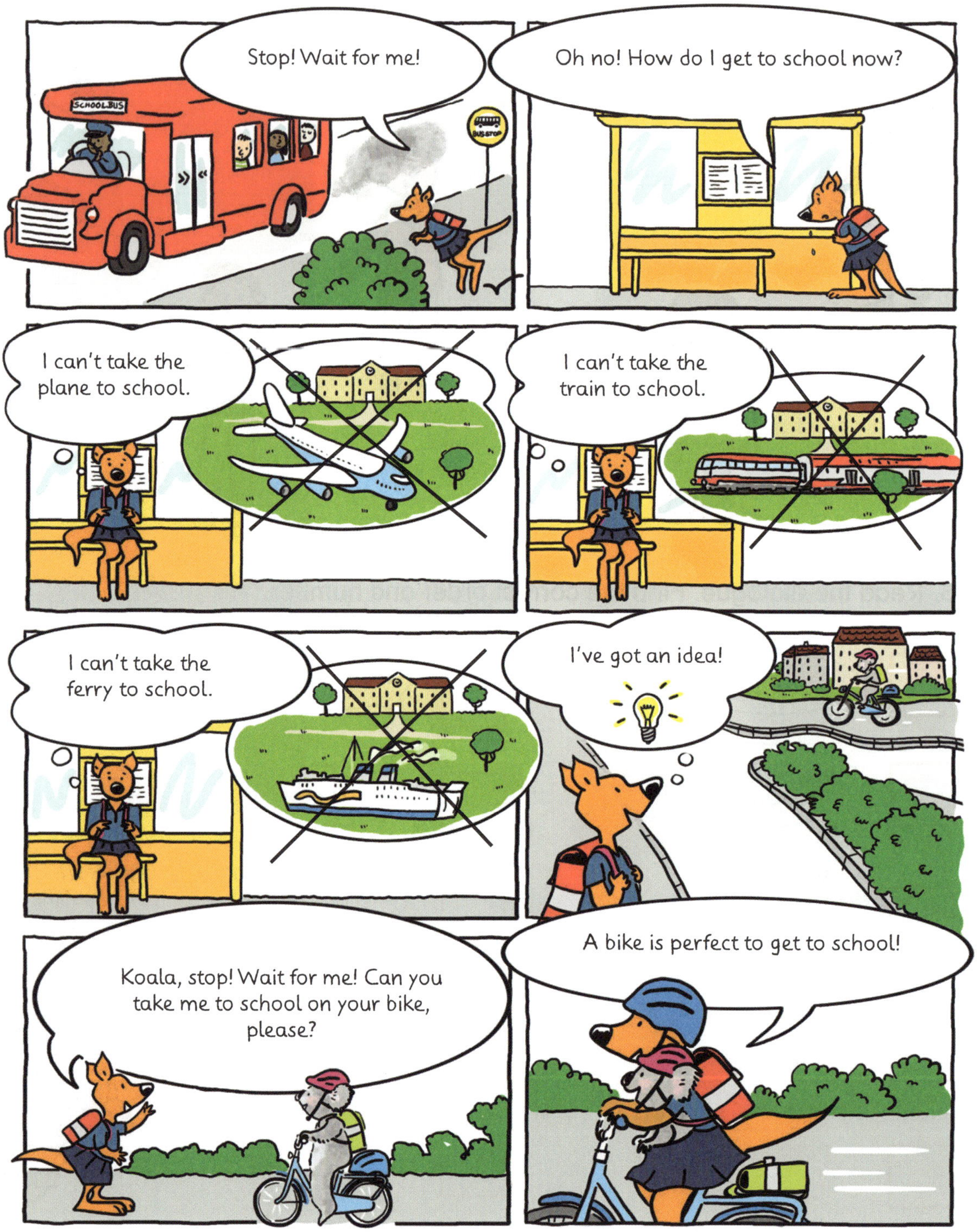

5. Fill in the speech bubbles.

It's too big.

I like it.

It's too small.

Welche Aussage passt zu welchem Bild? Trage in die Sprechblasen ein.

I don't like it.

6. Read the dialogue. Find the correct order and number.

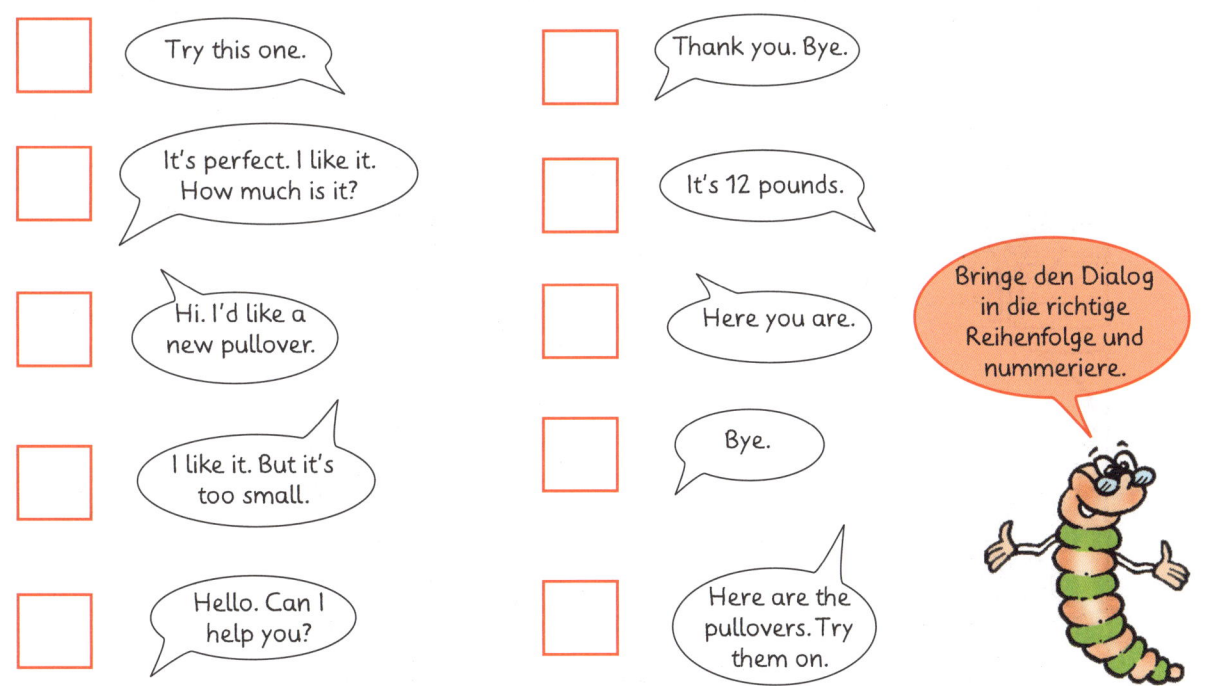

Try this one.

Thank you. Bye.

It's perfect. I like it. How much is it?

It's 12 pounds.

Hi. I'd like a new pullover.

Here you are.

I like it. But it's too small.

Bye.

Hello. Can I help you?

Here are the pullovers. Try them on.

Bringe den Dialog in die richtige Reihenfolge und nummeriere.

Comic

How do I get to school?

Stop! Wait for me!

Oh no! How do I get to school now?

I can't take the plane to school.

I can't take the train to school.

I can't take the ferry to school.

I've got an idea!

Koala, stop! Wait for me! Can you take me to school on your bike, please?

A bike is perfect to get to school!

1. Read the sentences. Fill in the gaps.

Sally is late. She misses the _____.

She can't get to school by plane, by _____

or by _____.

Sally's friend Koala gets to school by _____.

For Sally and Koala a bike is _____ to get to school.

2. Look at the picture. What different vehicles can you see? Count and write.

I can see [ ] cars _____ [ ] _____ [ ] _____

[ ] _____ [ ] _____ [ ] _____

[ ] _____ [ ] _____

Zähle die verschie-
denen Fahrzeuge
und schreibe auf.

bike   boat   bus – buses
car   ferry – ferries   plane
taxi   train   underground

to get to –
   hinkommen

to miss –
   verpassen

to take – nehmen

vehicle –
   Fahrzeug

to wait – warten

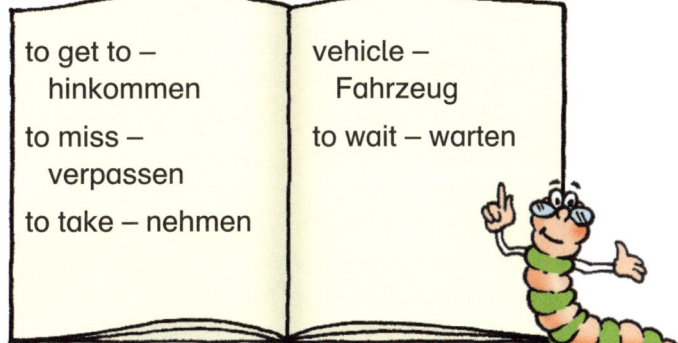

27

3. Look at the pictures. Write the sentences.

The fish gets to school by _____.

The dog gets _____.

The frog _____.

The hamster _____.

The cat _____.

The guinea pig _____.

Sally _____.

Wie kommen Sally und all die anderen Tiere in die Schule? Vervollständige die Sätze.

4. Make dialogues. Write.

How can I get to the cinema, please?

You can take the underground.

How can I get to the supermarket, please?

You can take the

_____.

_____

_____

_____

_____

_____

_____

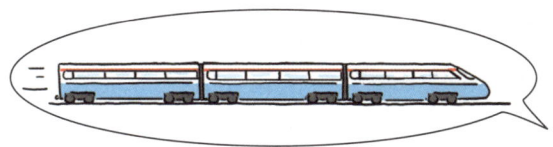 

_____

_____

🔖 👂 Comic

Good friends

A DAY IN THE JUNGLE

The tortoise is reading a book.

The fat hippo is swimming in the river.

The strong elephant is lifting heavy weights.

It's so boring here. Every day is the same.

The tall giraffe is eating leaves off the tree.

The dangerous lion is frightening the zebra. The fast zebra is running away.

The monkey is right. Every day is the same.

But what can we do?

I've got an idea.

THE NEXT DAY

The clever tortoise is eating leaves off the tree.

The hippo is reading a book and the giraffe is swimming in the river.

The long snake is lifting heavy weights.

Hey friends, what are you doing?

The fast zebra is frightening the dangerous lion. The dangerous lion is running away.

We want to make you laugh.

You are so crazy! You are my best friends!

30

 1. Look at the end of the comic. What are the animals doing? Read and draw lines.

The snake	is swimming in the river.
The giraffe	is eating leaves off the tree.
The lion	is reading a book.
The zebra	is running away.
The tortoise	is frightening the lion.
The hippo	is lifting heavy weights.

Two animals are missing. Write.

_____

animal   elephant
giraffe   hippo   jungle
lion   monkey   parrot
river   snake   tortoise
tree   zebra   clever
dangerous   fast   fat
funny   long   old
strong   tall
in   on   under

behind – hinter

boring – langweilig

to frighten – erschrecken

heavy – schwer

high – hoch

in front of – vor

leaves – Blätter

to lift – heben

to run away – wegrennen

sharp – scharf

to weigh – wiegen

weights – Gewichte

2. Read and find the adjective.

The elephant can lift about 300 kilogrammes.

The elephant is _____ .

| dangerous |
| old   tall |
| strong |
| fast   fat |

The hippo weighs about 1500 kilogrammes.

The hippo is _____ .

The zebra can run about 75 kilometres

per hour. The zebra is _____ .

The tortoise lives about 150 years.

The tortoise is _____ .

The lion has got sharp teeth.

The lion is _____ .

The giraffe is about 5 metres

high. The giraffe is _____ .

3. Which word is wrong? Cross it out.

The lion is the ~~banana~~ king of the jungle.

The elephant is in big and strong.

The crocodile is very hot dangerous.

The snake is very long hair.

The monkey likes to swing songs in the trees.

The tortoise drinks eats grass.

The hippo swims in the river salt.

The dog parrot flies from tree to tree.

 4. Where are the animals? Write.

in on under behind next to in front of

The monkey is in the tree.

The hippo is _____

_____

_____

_____

_____

_____

_____

33

Comic

Sally at the dentist

1. Read and circle the wrong word. Write the correct word.

I've got a ~~headache.~~
__toothache__

Open your nose.
_____

You have got a hole in your foot.
_____

Bacteria like the sugar on your mouth.
_____

Brush your hair at least in the morning and in the evening.
_____

Here is a shoe brush and toothpaste for you.
_____

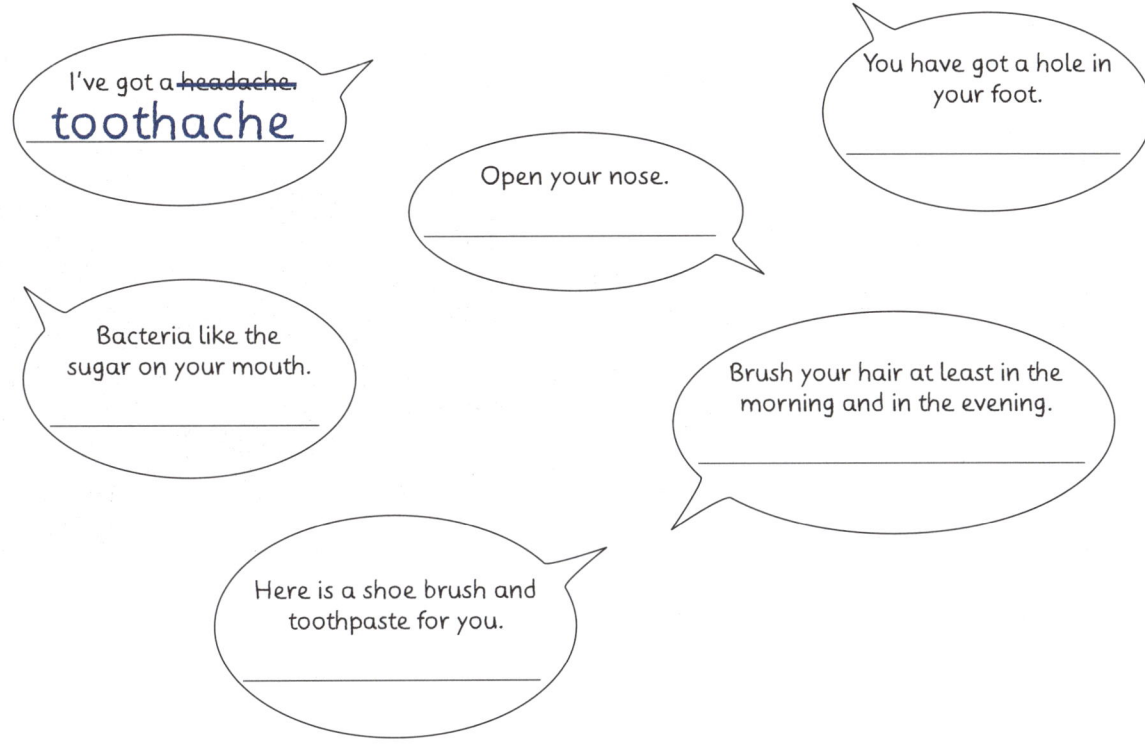

arm   broken   ear – earache   eye   finger   foot – feet

head – headache   to hurt   knee   leg   mouth   nose

to open   stomach – stomachache   throat – sore throat

tooth – teeth   toothache   What's the matter?

bacteria – Bakterien

to brush – bürsten

hole – Loch

toothbrush – Zahnbürste

toothpaste – Zahnpasta

Achte auf den unregel-mäßigen Plural:
one tooth – two teeth
one foot – two feet

🔍 ✏️ 2. Find the 6 differences. Circle and write.

In picture 1 the zebra has got a headache. In picture 2 the zebra has got a stomachache.

In picture 1 the hippo has got a toothache. In picture 2 _____

_____

_____

_____

_____

_____

_____

_____

_____

_____

3. What's the matter? Look and write.

   I've got a _____.

   My _____ hurts.

   I've got a _____.

    My _____ hurts.

 4. Read and number in the correct order.

☐   Is my leg broken?

☐   My leg hurts.

☐   Thank you Doctor Miller.

☐   Okay, let's see.

☐   No, your leg isn't broken. Let's put some ice on it.

☐   See you again next week.

☐   What's the matter with you?

 Comic

A long day

It's 3.30 in the afternoon.

That was a long school day. And now I have to do my homework.

Rrrring!

Oscar, can you please walk the dog?

Okay, Dad.

It's 4.30.

I have to do my homework now.

Oscar, can you please help me clean the kitchen before Mum gets home? It looks like a mess.

Okay, I can help you.

It's 5.30.

I really have to do my homework now.

Oh no. I have to feed the cat now.

Meow!

Hi Oscar. Why are you still doing your homework? It's already 6 o'clock. Did you play football all afternoon?

Mum, you have no idea.

1. True or false? Tick ✓.

	true	false
Oscar has to do his homework.	◯	◯
Oscar has to make his bed.	◯	◯
Oscar has to help in the garden.	◯	◯
Oscar has to take the cat for a walk.	◯	◯
Oscar has to clean the kitchen.	◯	◯
Oscar has to feed the cat.	◯	◯
Oscar plays football in the afternoon.	◯	◯

doctor   gardener   hairdresser   pilot
policeman / policewoman   shop assistant
teacher   to babysit   to do homework
to feed the cat   to help in the garden
to make breakfast
to make my bed   to tidy my room
to walk the dog   to work

to have to –
    müssen

late – spät

mess –
    Durcheinander

You have no
    idea! – Du hast
    keine Ahnung!

 2. What do these children have to do in the house? Look and write.

I have to
_____
_____ .

I have to
_____
_____ .

I have to
_____
_____ .

I have to
_____
_____ .

I have to
_____
_____ .

3. What are their jobs? Find the words.

I'm a _____ .

radesrehsri

I'm a _____ .

lmcipnoea

I'm a _____ .

otipl

I'm a _____ .

acereht

40

✎ 4. Where do they work? Draw lines and write.

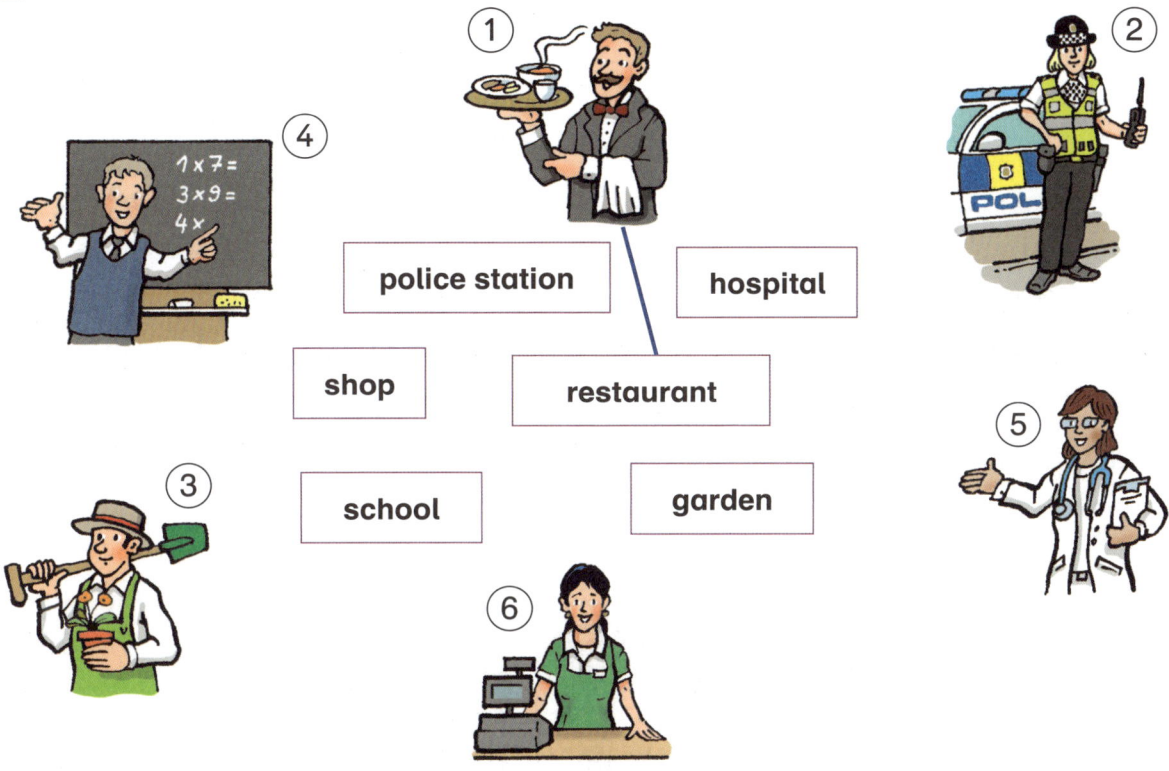

① The waiter works at the restaurant.

② _____

③ _____

④ _____

⑤ _____

⑥ _____

🖌✎ 5. What do you want to be? Draw and write.

I want to be a

_____

Comic

The new pupil

1. Look at the comic. Write the countries.

Finde die Länder zu diesen Hauptstädten.

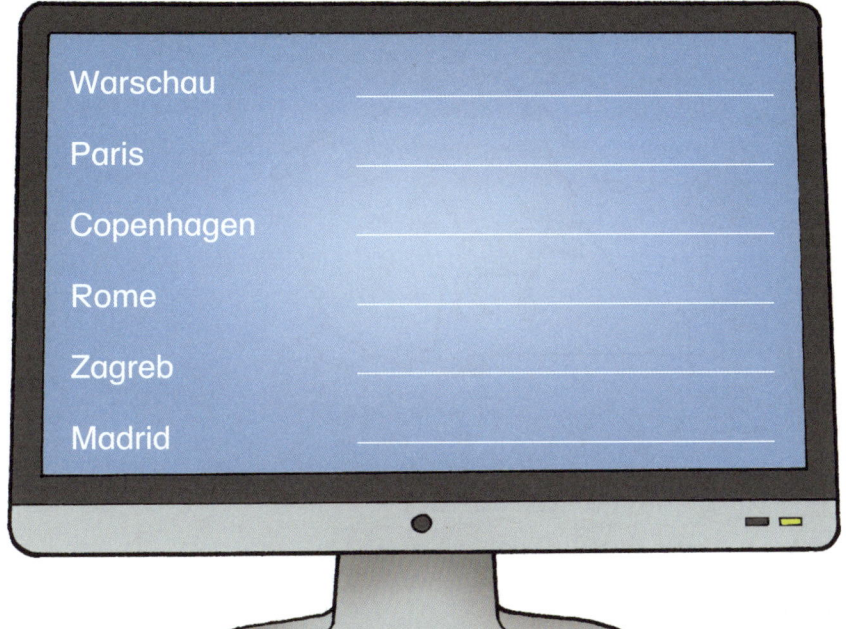

Warschau _____

Paris _____

Copenhagen _____

Rome _____

Zagreb _____

Madrid _____

Dimitri is from _____. The capital city is _____.

capital city   city – cities   country – countries   Croatia   Denmark
England   France   Germany   Great Britain   Greece   Italy
Poland   Spain   Sweden   Turkey   English   French   German
Greek   Spanish   Turkish   Ankara   Athens   Berlin   Copenhagen
London   Madrid   Paris   Rome   Stockholm   Warschau   Zagreb
Where are you from? – I'm from ...
Which languages can you speak? – I (can) speak ...

Kennst du die Länder und ihre Hauptstädte? Die Abbildungen, die typisch für die entsprechenden Länder sind helfen dir dabei.

🖊 2. Do you know these countries? Write.

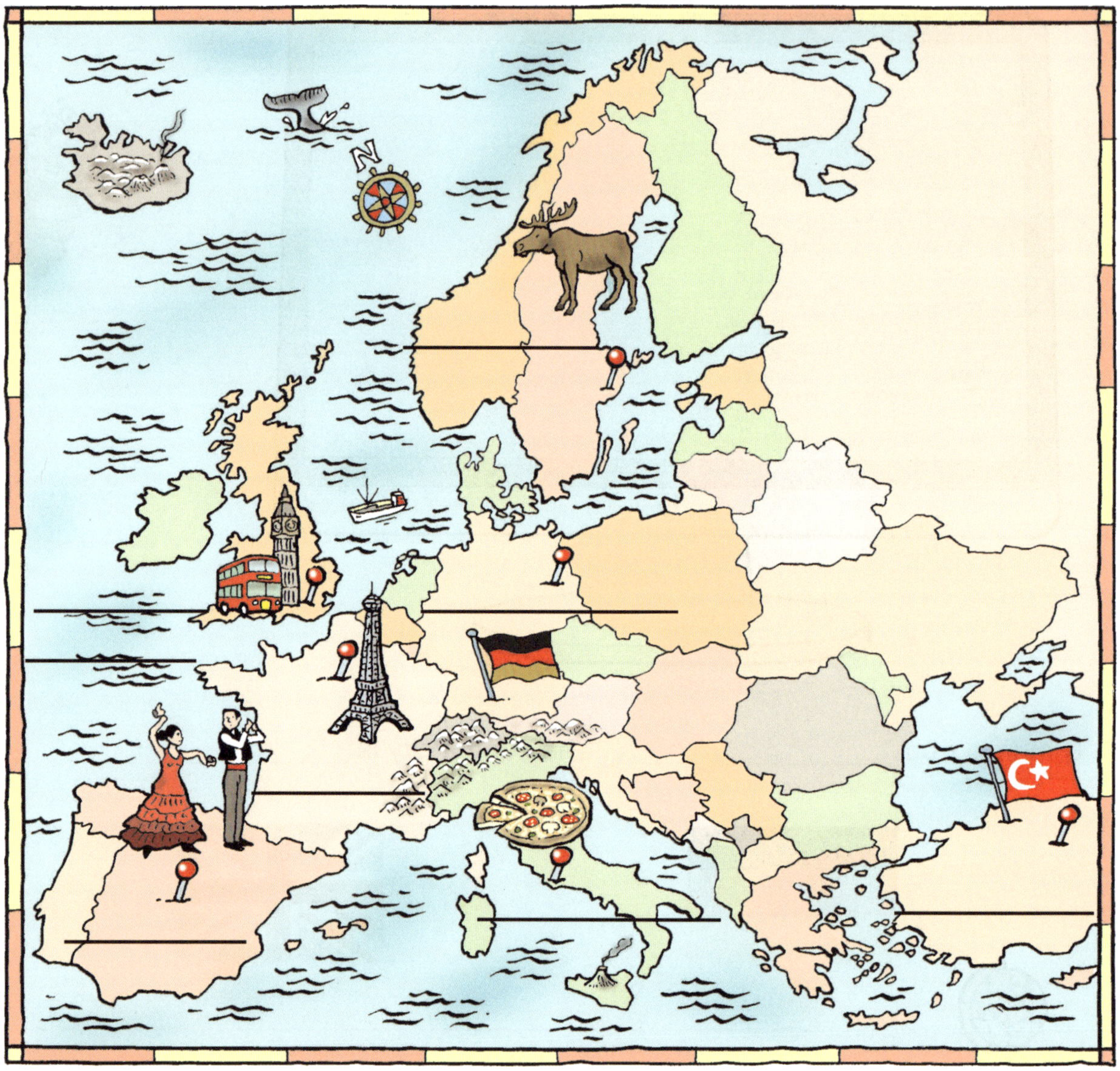

What are their capital cities?

44

4. Which languages do the children speak? Write.

Hi. I'm Susana. I'm from Sp__ __ __. I speak

S p a n i s h.

Hi. I'm Tom. I'm from E_ _ _ _ _ _ _. I speak _ _ _ _ _ _ _ _.

My name is Burak. I'm from T_ _ _ _ _ _. I speak _ _ _ _ _ _ _ _.

Bonjour! My name is Celine. I'm from F_ _ _ _ _ _. I speak _ _ _ _ _ _ _.

Now it's your turn.

My name is _____. I'm from _____. I speak

_____. I can also speak _____.

5. Read. Colour the question and the correct answer in the same colour.

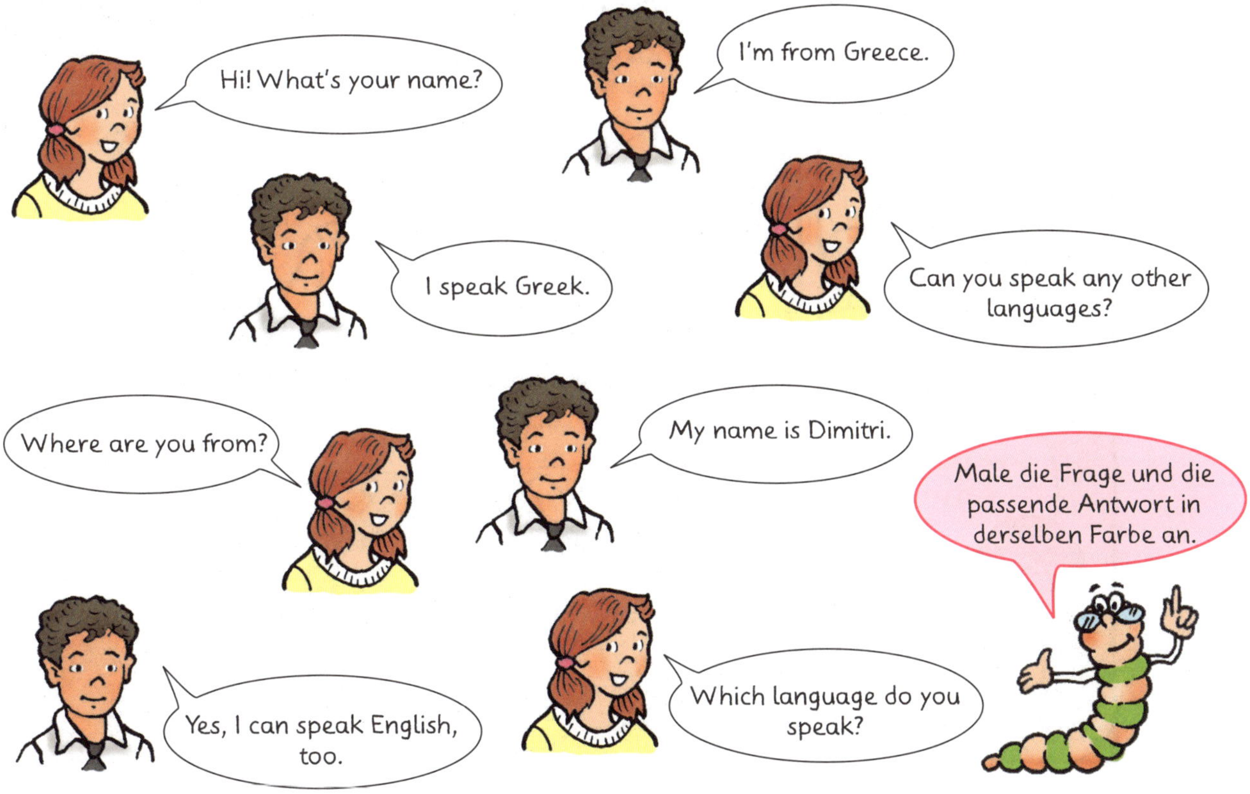

Hi! What's your name?

I'm from Greece.

I speak Greek.

Can you speak any other languages?

Where are you from?

My name is Dimitri.

Male die Frage und die passende Antwort in derselben Farbe an.

Yes, I can speak English, too.

Which language do you speak?

45

 Comic

The Little Indian Boy

Once upon a time there lived an Indian family in a tepee, an Indian tent.

They all had Indian names.

My name is Singing Bird. I love to sing.

And my name is Fast Horse. I can run very fast.

My name is Little Rainbow because I love colours.

I'm strong like a bear. That's why my name is Strong Bear.

Our baby is born! Come here everybody. Our little boy needs a name.

Little Rainbow and Strong Bear had a little baby boy.

Was it a dark night when he was born?

No!

Was it snowy and cold when he was born?

No!

Was it rainy or cloudy when he was born?

No!

But the sun was shining when he was born. That's a perfect name for our little boy: Shining Sun!

Welcome to our family, Shining Sun!

46

 1. Read and tick ✓ the correct answer.

What is a tepee?

☐ It's an Indian tent. ☐ It's an Indian horse.

Whose name is Fast Horse?

☐ It's Grandma's name. ☐ It's Grandpa's name.

Why is Dads's name Strong Bear?

☐ Because he is strong like a bear. ☐ Because he is brown like a bear.

What was the weather like when the little boy was born?

☐ It was a cold and dark night. ☐ It was a warm and sunny day.

Ein indianischer Name hatte immer eine besondere Bedeutung. Er richtete sich z.B. nach einer körperlichen Eigenschaft, einer Ähnlichkeit mit einer Pflanze oder einem Tier oder aber nach einem Wetterereignis am Tag der Geburt.

American football

California   cowboy   Florida

Hollywood   Indian

New York

president   ranch

Statue of Liberty

White House

background – Hintergrund

to be born – geboren werden

famous – berühmt

popular – beliebt

president – Präsident

stripes – Streifen

tent – Zelt

tepee – Indianerzelt

 5. Look at the pictures. Read and number.

① Hollywood is the home of many famous film stars.

② The president of the USA lives in the White House in Washington DC.

③ In Florida there are beautiful beaches where you can swim and surf.

④ American football is a popular sport in the USA.

⑤ The Statue of Liberty is in New York.

⑥ The biggest trees in the world are in California.

⑦ A cowboy works on a ranch.

6. Read and colour the American flag.

The American flag has got
white stars
on a blue background.
The stripes are red and white.

Die Sterne in der amerikanischen Flagge stehen für die Staaten. Es sind 50 Sterne, ein Stern für jeden Staat. Die 13 roten und weißen Streifen stehen für die Ursprungskolonien.